BASS RECORDED VERSIONS

THE Stanley Clarke COLLECTION

Front cover photo by Neil Zlozower

Music transcriptions by Chris Kringel, Jeff Jacobson and Matt Scharfglass

ISBN 0-7935-4443-2

HAL•LEONARD®
CORPORATION

7777 W. BLUEMOUND RD. P.O. BOX 13819 MILWAUKEE, WI 53213

For all works contained herein:
Unauthorized copying, arranging, adapting, recording or public performance is an infringement of copyright.
Infringers are liable under the law.

Visit Hal Leonard Online at
www.halleonard.com

Photo by Neil Zlozower

Stanley Clarke

Performer, Bandleader, Arranger, Producer and Composer

Stanley Clarke is one of the most celebrated bassists in the world today. During his career, he has received virtually every honor that can be bestowed upon a musician, including *Rolling Stone*'s "Jazzman of the Year," *Playboy* magazine, "Jazz Bassist of the Year" for ten consecutive years, and *Guitar Player* magazine's "Gallery of Greats." A seven-time Grammy nominee, Clarke received a Grammy for his critically-acclaimed album *No Mystery* in 1975 and his score for *Boyz N The Hood* received an Oscar nomination. In 1989, he returned to his native Philadelphia where his name was placed in cement on the "Walk of Fame," and where Mayor Wilson Goode presented him with a Philadelphia Music Foundation *Hall of Fame* award. His albums continue to top a variety of charts; not only Jazz, but the R&B, New Adult Contemporary and Top Pop charts.

Born in 1951, Clarke was encouraged from an early age to study music by his mother, who sang opera. Though he initially studied violin and cello, he literally outgrew both instruments. With his long, lean frame, he was a natural to play the acoustic bass. Equally interested in jazz, classical, and rock music, Clarke started playing in bands in junior high. By the time he'd reached the twelfth grade he became a serious student of the bass, practicing and playing for eight hours a day. At 16, he bought an electric bass for $29.00, a Kent hollow body, so he could get after-school jobs playing bass. His jobs ranged from a blues combo, a country group and a Top-40 band that rolled into the Holiday Inn circuit. He then enrolled in the prestigious Philadelphia Musical Academy, studying string bass and composition, but continuing to be influenced by Jimi Hendrix, Jack Bruce and Charles Mingus, as well as Bach, Beethoven and Wagner.

In 1970, Clarke moved to New York City where he played with such jazz greats as Horace Silver, Stan Getz, Dexter Gordon, Art Blakey, and Gil Evans. He came into international prominence as a founding member of the groundbreaking jazz-rock fusion band, Return to Forever. Though initially a jazz purist devoted exclusively to the acoustic bass, Clarke went electric and electrified the music world during his eight-album collaboration with members Chick Corea, Lenny White and Al Di Meola. In 1975, Return to Forever's *No Mystery* album won the Grammy for Best Jazz Performance by a Group. His slap and pop playing with this group had a powerful influence on the jazz-funk styles to come.

Clarke remembers those times: "The Return to Forever years were important for me... RTF was really one of the only times in my playing career that I got to use some of the skills I'd worked on in college—through composition, writing for orchestra and things like that. Because before we did an album, we'd always take off for a month or so to compose music."

During his tenure with Return to Forever, Clarke launched his highly-successful solo career. On his 1972 solo album, *Children of Forever*, he played acoustic exclusively. The 1975 release of *Stanley Clarke* with Tony Williams and Jan Hammer put him into the fusion scene. His 1976 album *School Days* became a crossover hit. His crossover R&B/pop Clarke/Duke Project in collaboration with keyboardist George Duke resulted in three best-selling albums and a Top 20 single, "Sweet Baby." Their 1990 album *3* garnered the duo an NAACP Image Award nomination for Best Jazz Artists. His solo *East River Drive* featured an all-star ensemble including Duke, Hubert Laws, Jean-Luc Ponty, Poncho Sanchez and Gerald Albright, plus big names in bass: Abe Laboriel, Armand Sabal-Lecco, Alphonso Johnson and Jimmy Earl. Clarke's independent label, Slamm Dunk Records, has released a variety of recordings including his own *Live at the Greek*, and the soundtrack album for *Passenger 57*. *Live at the Greek* features Clarke with Larry Carlton, Billy Cobham and Najee.

Clarke's rock projects included working with Jeff Beck, Stewart Copeland, and Deborah Holland with the group Animal Logic, the New Barbarians (which featured The Rolling Stones' Ron Wood and Keith Richards) and scoring the opening sequence of Michael Jackson's video *Remember the Time*, which was directed by John Singleton. He has co-written with Paul McCartney, recorded with Quincy Jones, Carlos Santana and Aretha Franklin, and produced records for Brenda Russell, Ramsey Lewis, Shalamar, and Natalie Cole.

In the television arena Clarke has received three Emmy nominations for television scoring. He started out by sending tapes to everyone in the field, and got his first break doing *Pee-Wee's Playhouse*. That's when he bought his first Mac and MIDI keyboard, and got his first Emmy nomination. It was while scoring an episode of *Tales from the Crypt* that his desire to score was fueled, when he became aware of how powerful music can be in a scene.

With this turn in composing, Clarke has been in constant demand to score films and television since the mid '80s. His films include John Singleton's *Boyz N The Hood*, *Panther*, *Passenger 57*, *Book of Love*, *Poetic Justice*, *Higher Learning*, *Little Big League*, *Tap*, *Dangerous Ground*, *Cherokee Kidd*, and the acclaimed score for *What's Love Got To Do With It*, the drama based on the life of Tina Turner. He loves the challenge of composition and orchestration, the exposure to rapidly changing music technology, and the new sense of freedom, noting that "Underscoring, in particular, takes away all the constraints of producing music that must have commercial potential."

Clarke claims that film composing has influenced his solo writing—"When you do as much film composing as I've done lately, you just kind of get oiled as far as writing melodically is concerned."

Bass Folk Song

By Stanley Clarke

Copyright © 1973 (Renewed) Clarkee Music
All Rights Reserved

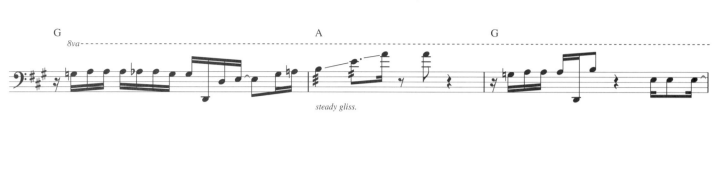

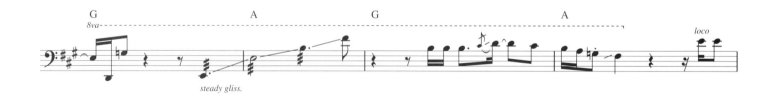

* Played behind the beat.

Christmas in Rio

By Stanley Clarke

*Tenor Bass Tuning:
(low to high) A–D–G–C

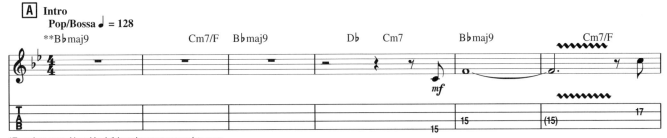

*Tenor bass notated in treble clef throughout to accommodate range.
**Chord symbols reflect overall tonality.

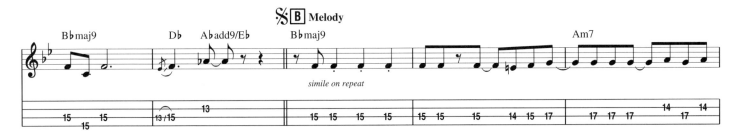

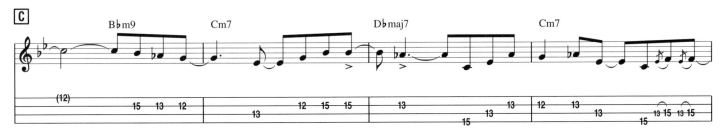

Copyright © 1993 Clarkee Music
All Rights Reserved

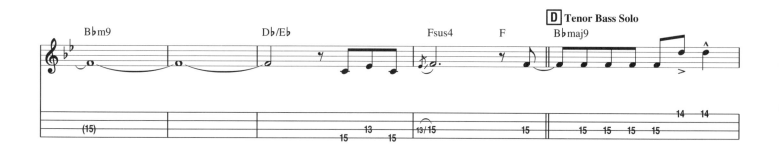

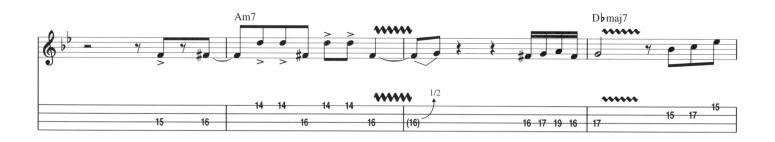

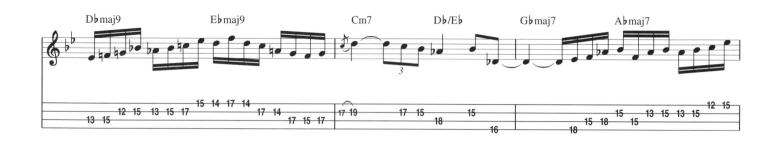

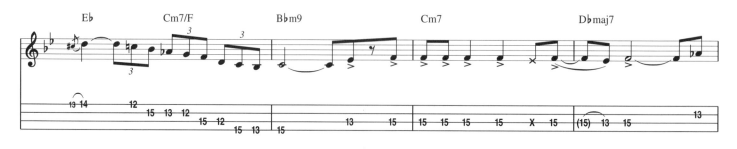

Dayride

By Stanley Clarke

Copyright © 1977 Clarkee Music
All Rights Reserved

* Notes in parentheses indicate synth arr. for bass.

East River Drive

By Stanley Clarke

Copyright © 1993 Clarkee Music
All Rights Reserved

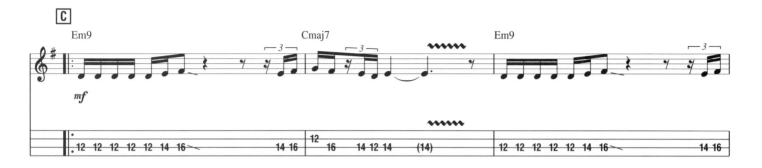

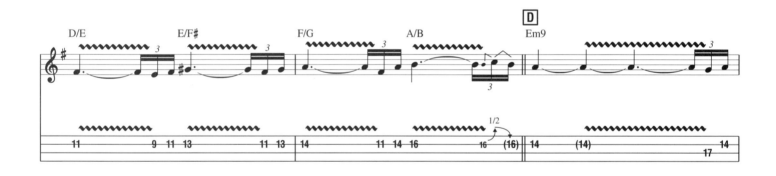

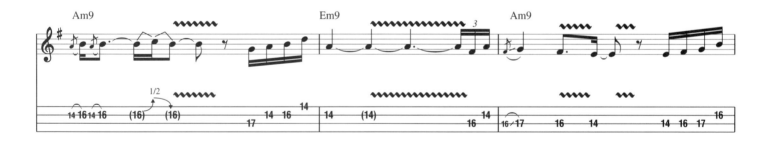

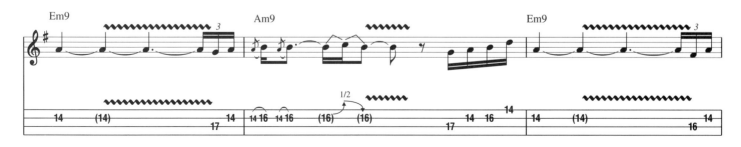

* Refers to upstemmed notes only.

* Bend neck to achieve vibrato.

I Wanna Play for You

By Stanley Clarke

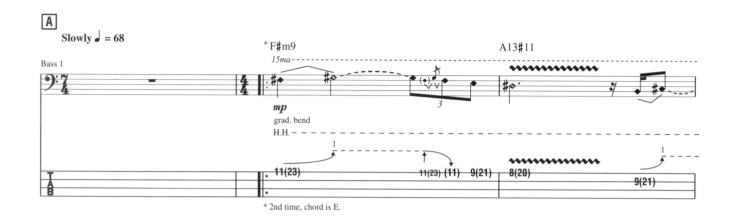

* 2nd time, chord is E.

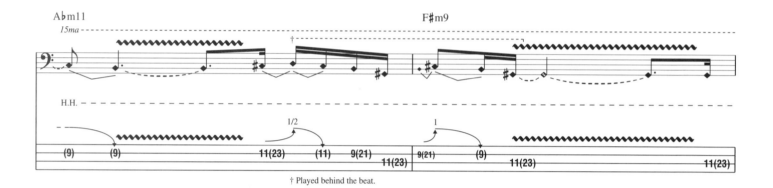

† Played behind the beat.

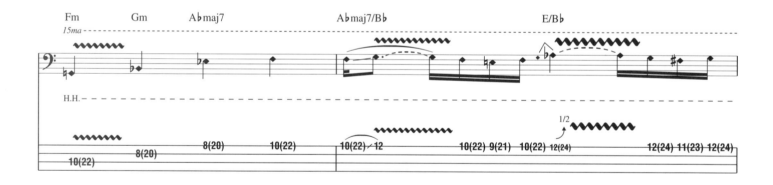

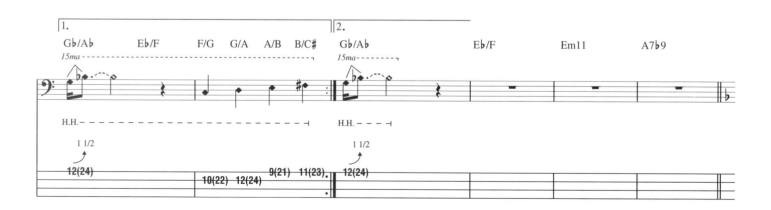

Copyright © 1979 Clarkee Music
All Rights Reserved

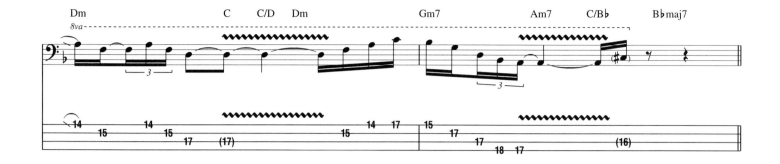

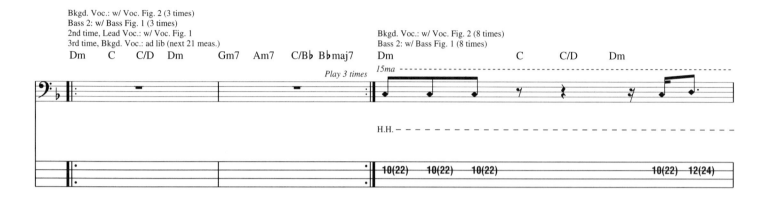

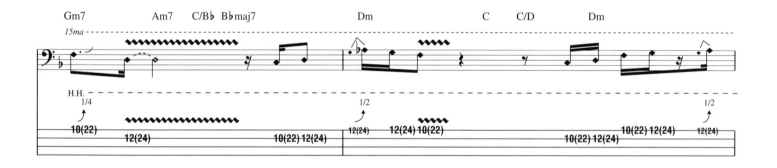

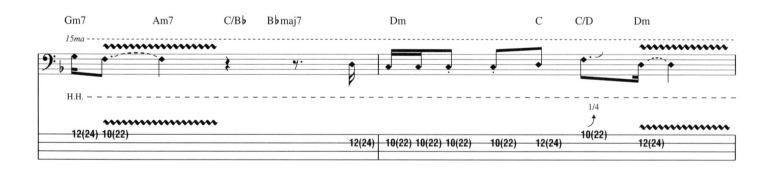

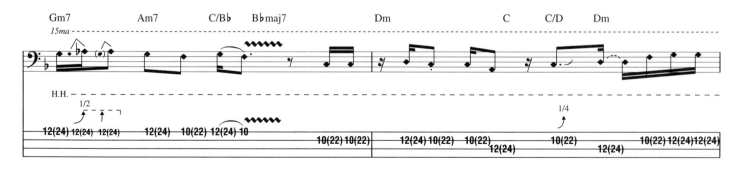

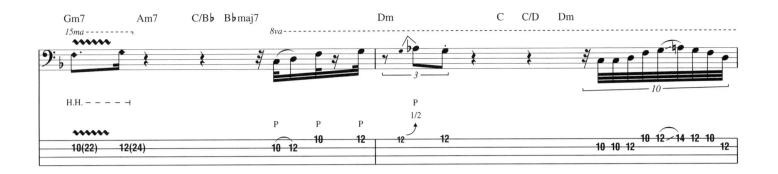

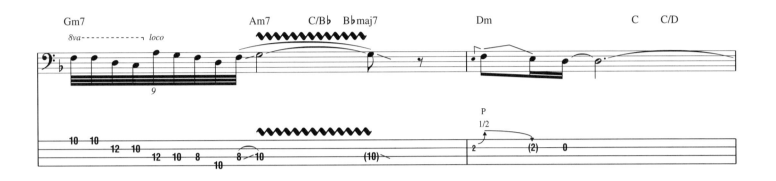

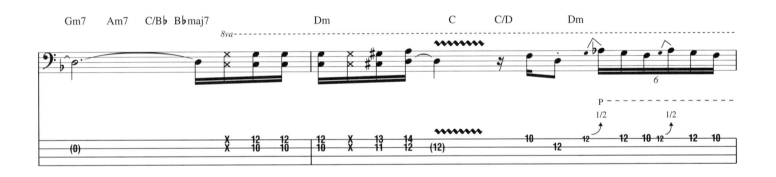

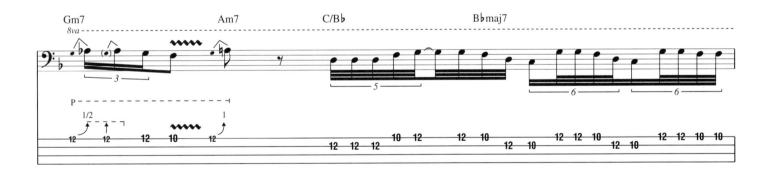

Bkgd. Voc.: w/ Voc. Fig. 2 (2 times)
Bass 2: w/ Bass Fig. 1 (2 times)

* Played behind the beat.

* Fret numbers above 24 are imaginary and are located past fretboard.

Life Is Just a Game

By Stanley Clarke

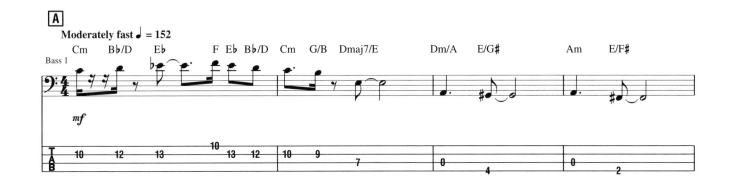

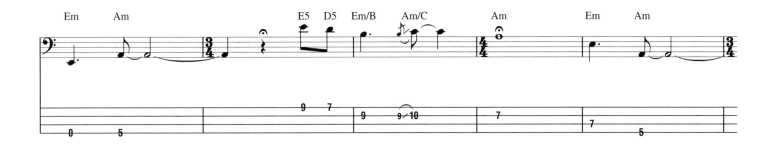

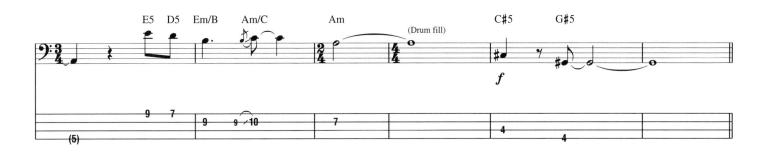

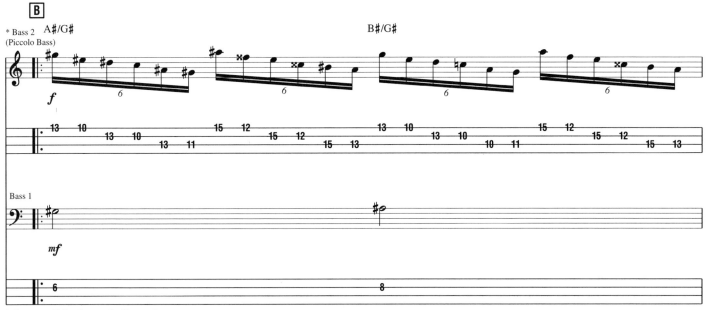

* One octave higher than standard bass tuning.

Copyright © 1976 Clarkee Music
All Rights Reserved

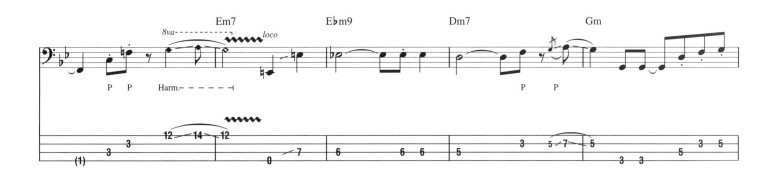

So life is ___ just a game and there's man - y ways to

play, ___ and all you do ___ is choose. ___

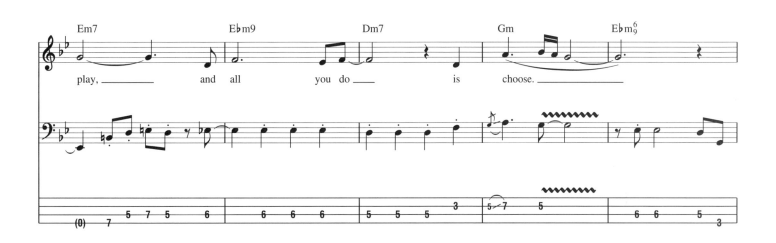

La, la, la, la, la. ___ La, la, ___

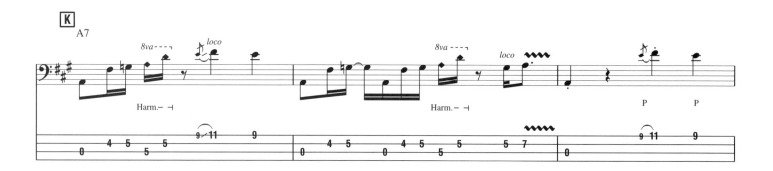

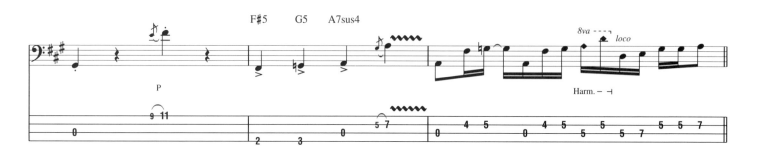

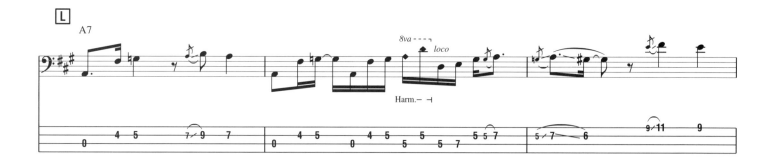

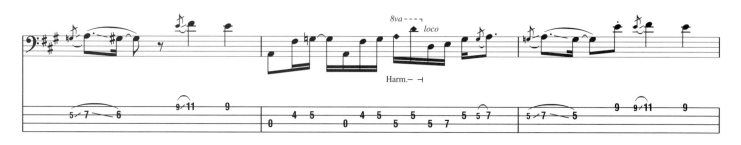

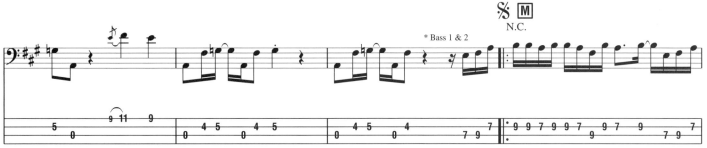

* Doubled an octave higher by piccolo bass (next 8 1/4 meas.)
Use same fingering.

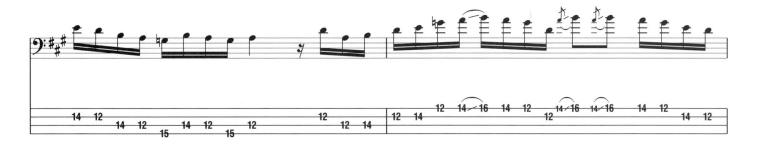

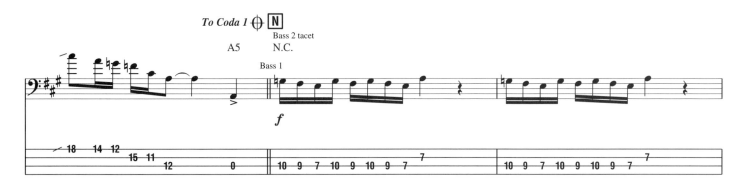

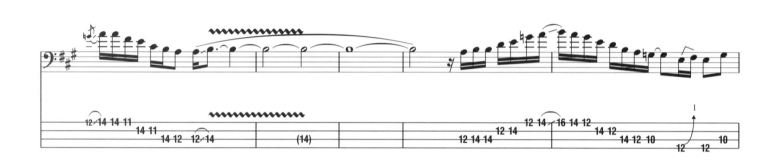

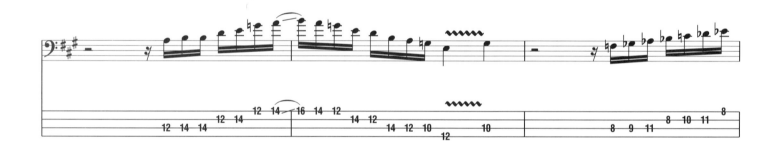

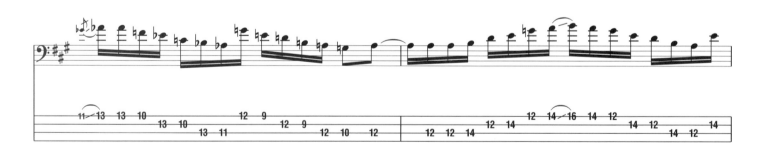

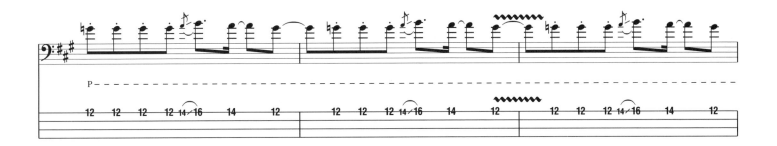

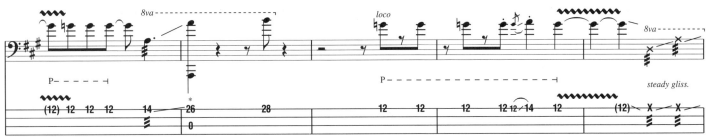

* Fret numbers above 24 are imaginary and are located past fretboard.

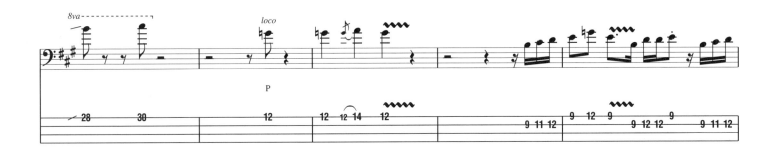

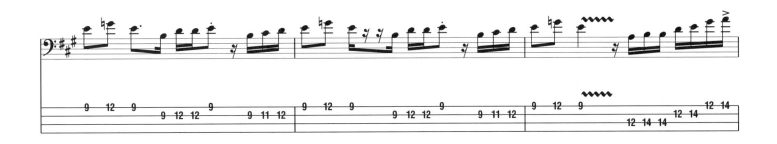

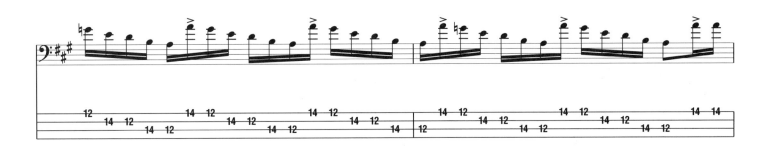

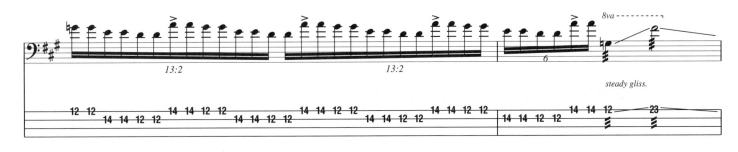

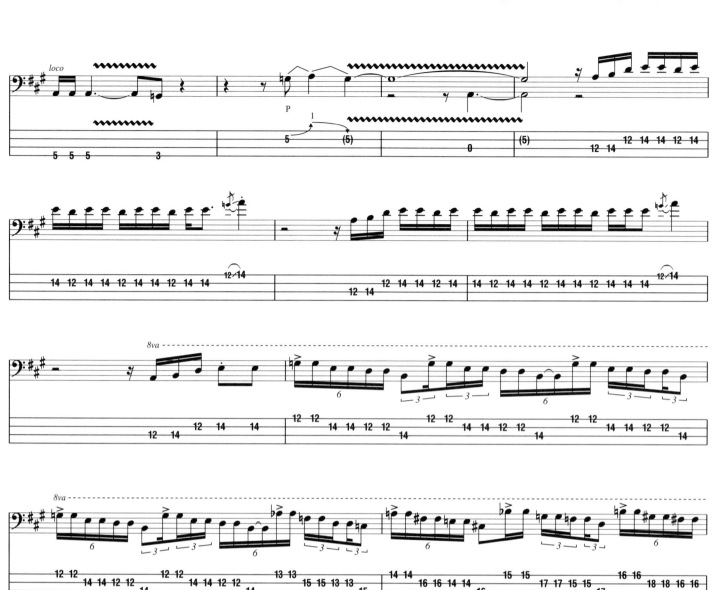

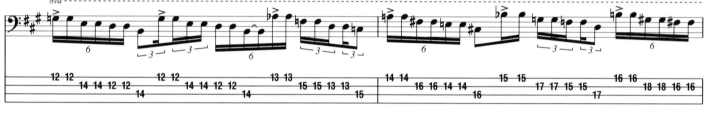

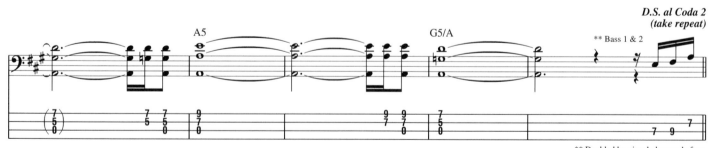

* Strum chords w/ R.H. fingers (next 6 meas.)

D.S. al Coda 2
(take repeat)

** Doubled by piccolo bass as before.

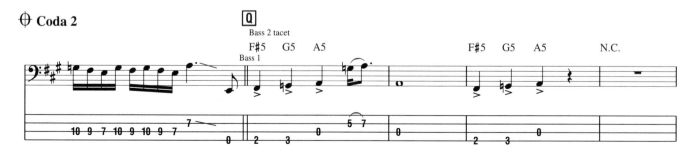

⊕ **Coda 2**

44

Lopsy Lu

By Stanley Clarke

* Mute open strings with left hand.

w/ fingers

To Coda ⊕

Copyright © 1977 Clarkee Music
All Rights Reserved

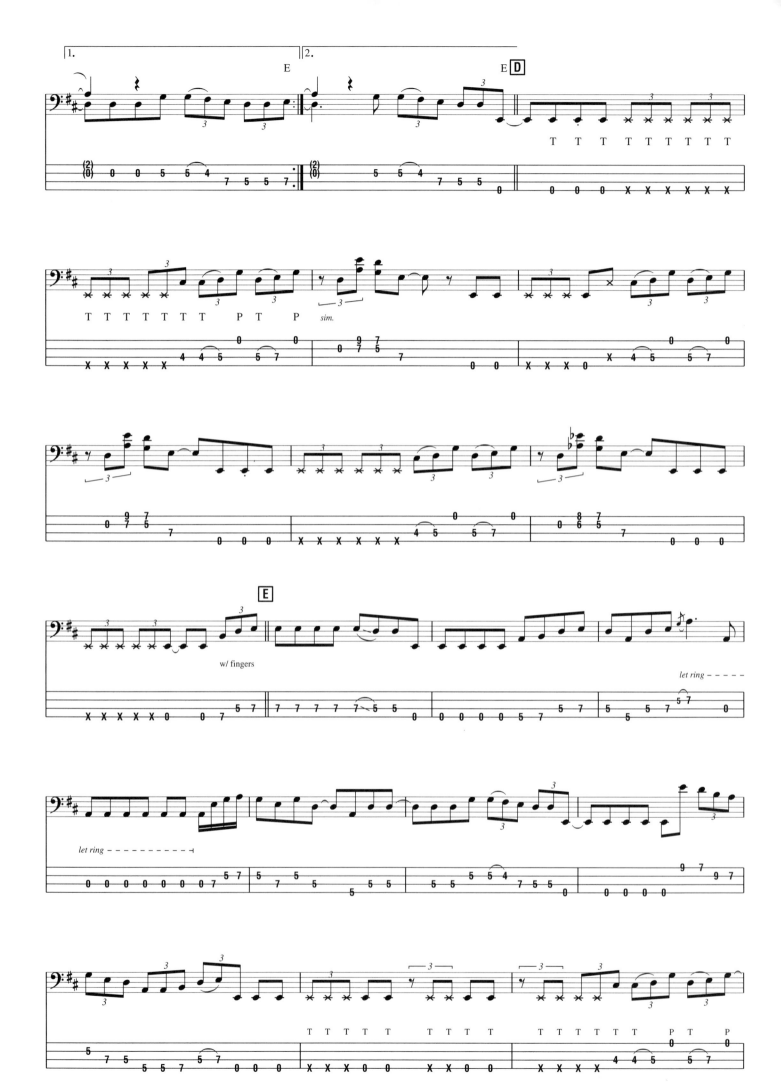

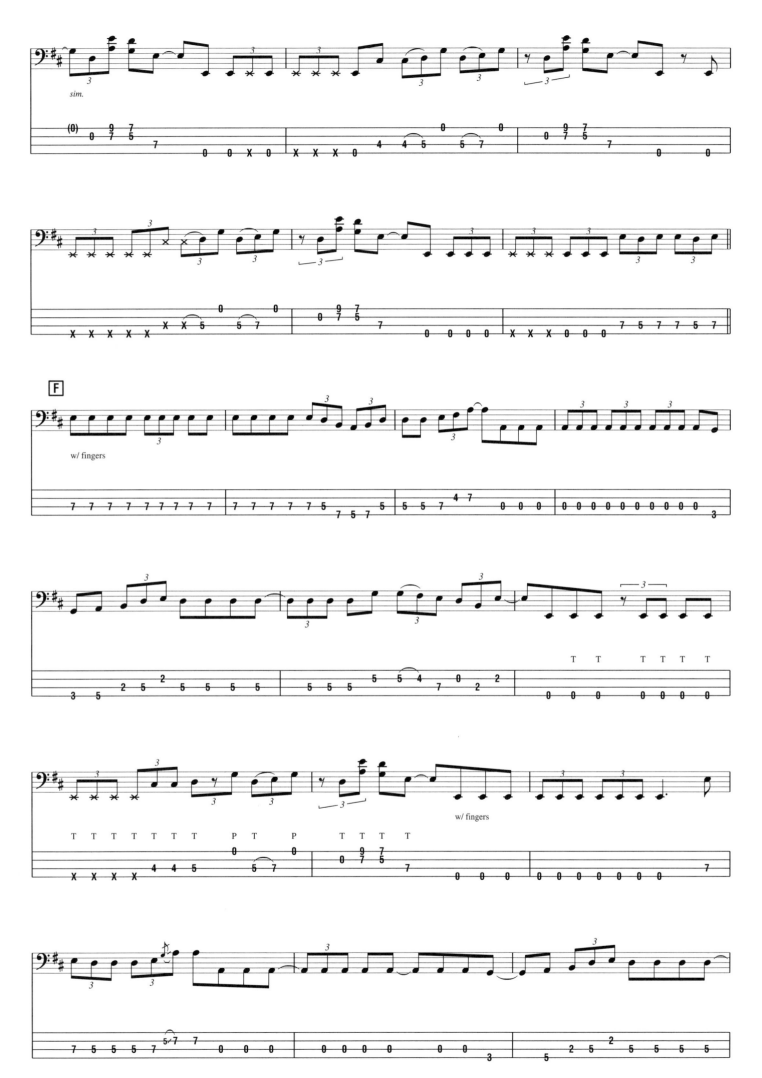

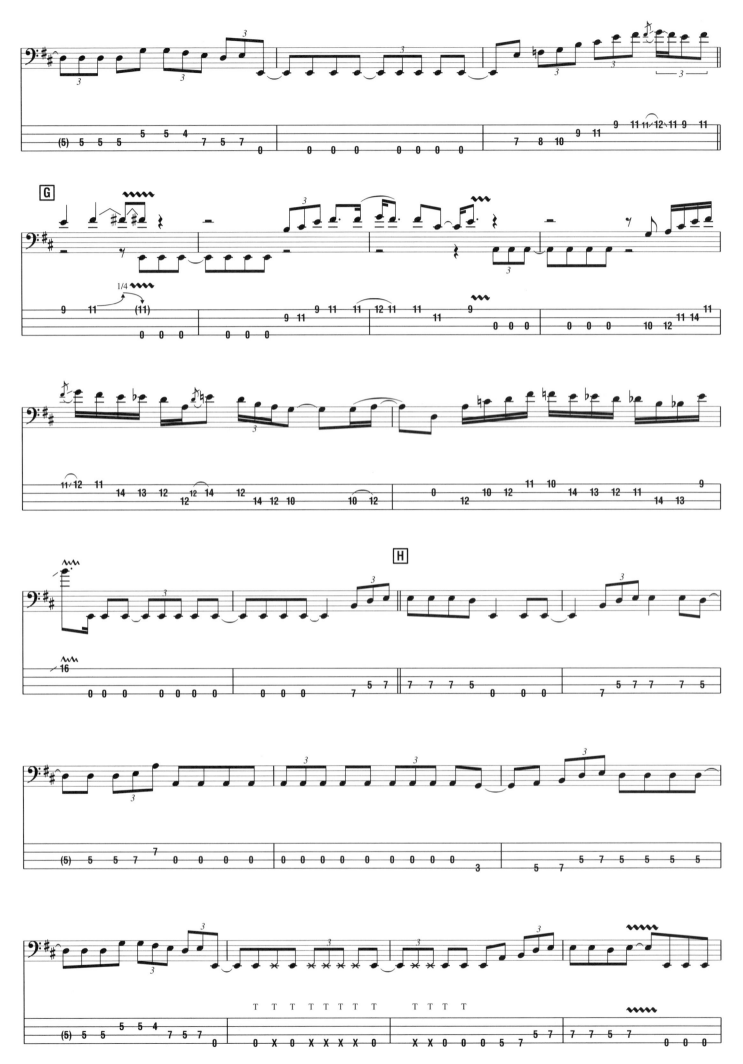

Coda

* Vibrato achieved by pulling and pushing on bass headstock.

** Bend achieved by pulling back on bass headstock or tightening tuning peg.

Fade out

The Magician

By Stanley Clarke

Copyright © 1976 Clarkee Music
All Rights Reserved

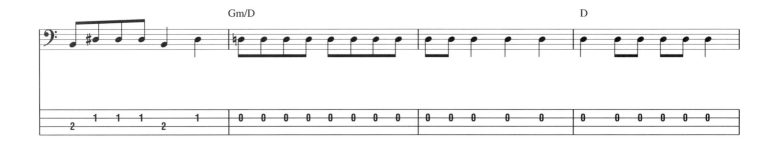

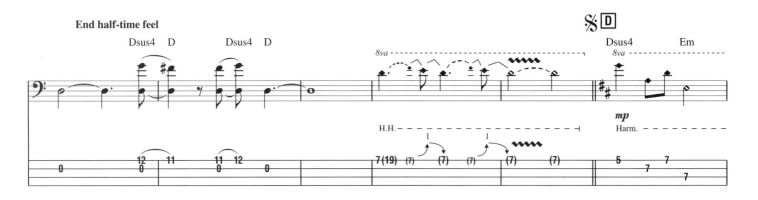

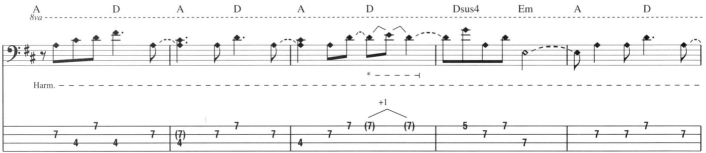

*Change in pitch achieved by bending neck, pushing down on string behind nut, or with bar.

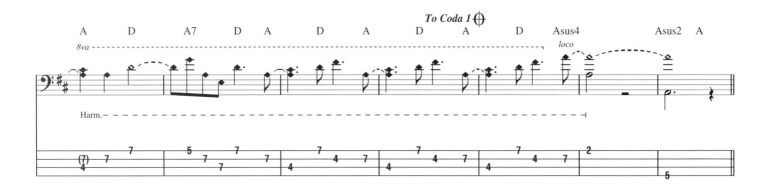

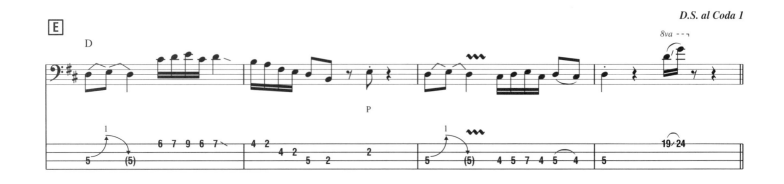

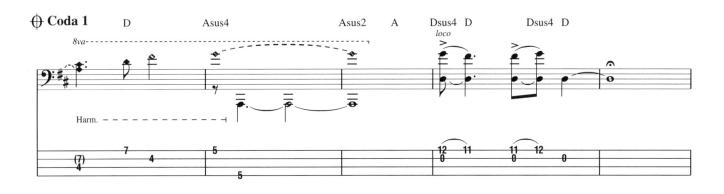

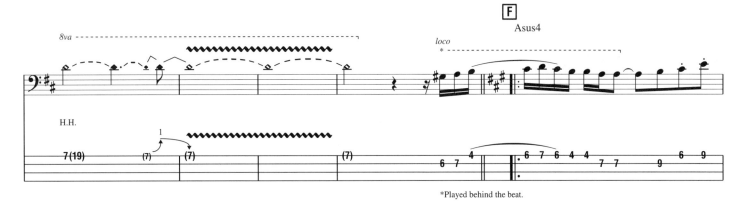

*Played behind the beat.

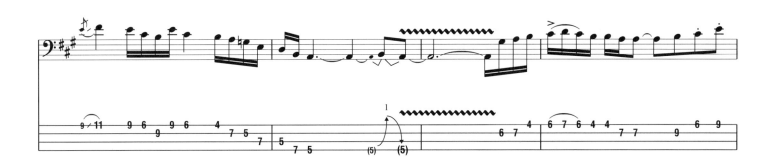

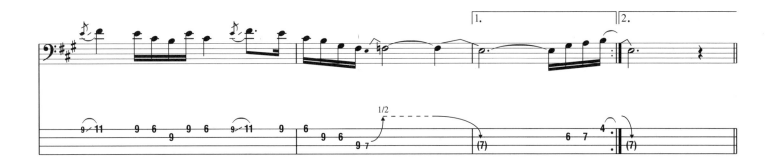

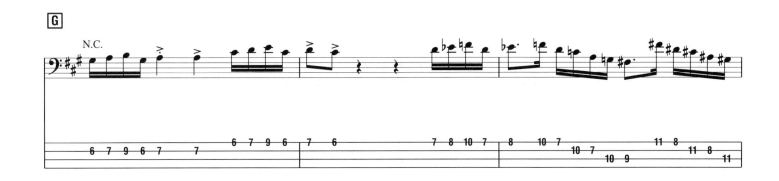

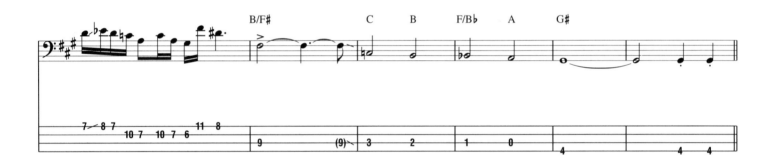

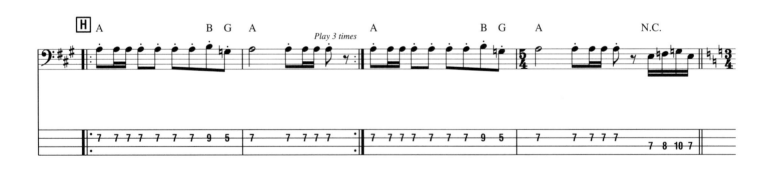

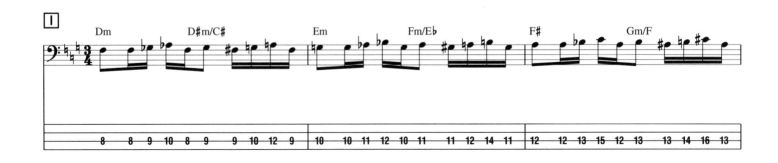

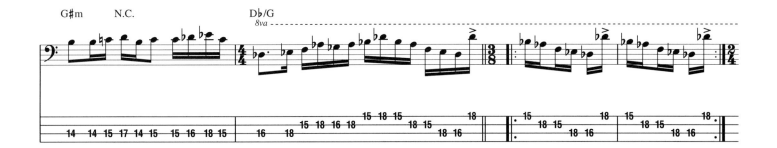

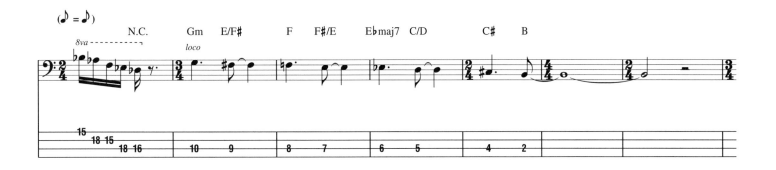

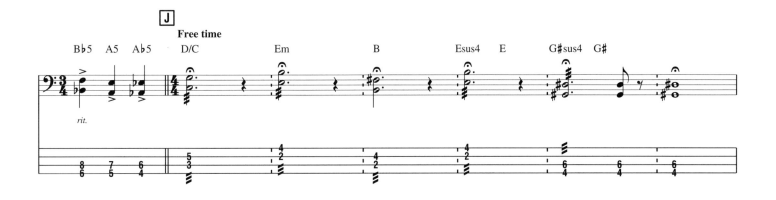

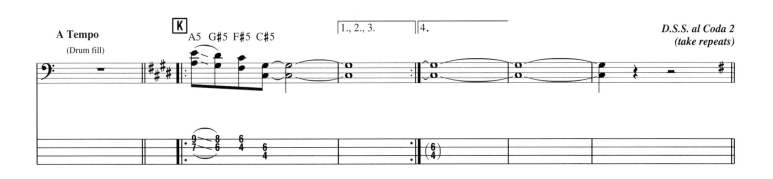

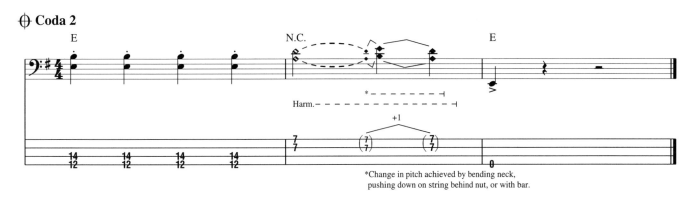

*Change in pitch achieved by bending neck,
pushing down on string behind nut, or with bar.

Rock 'n' Roll Jelly

By Stanley Clarke

Copyright © 1978 Clarkee Music
All Rights Reserved

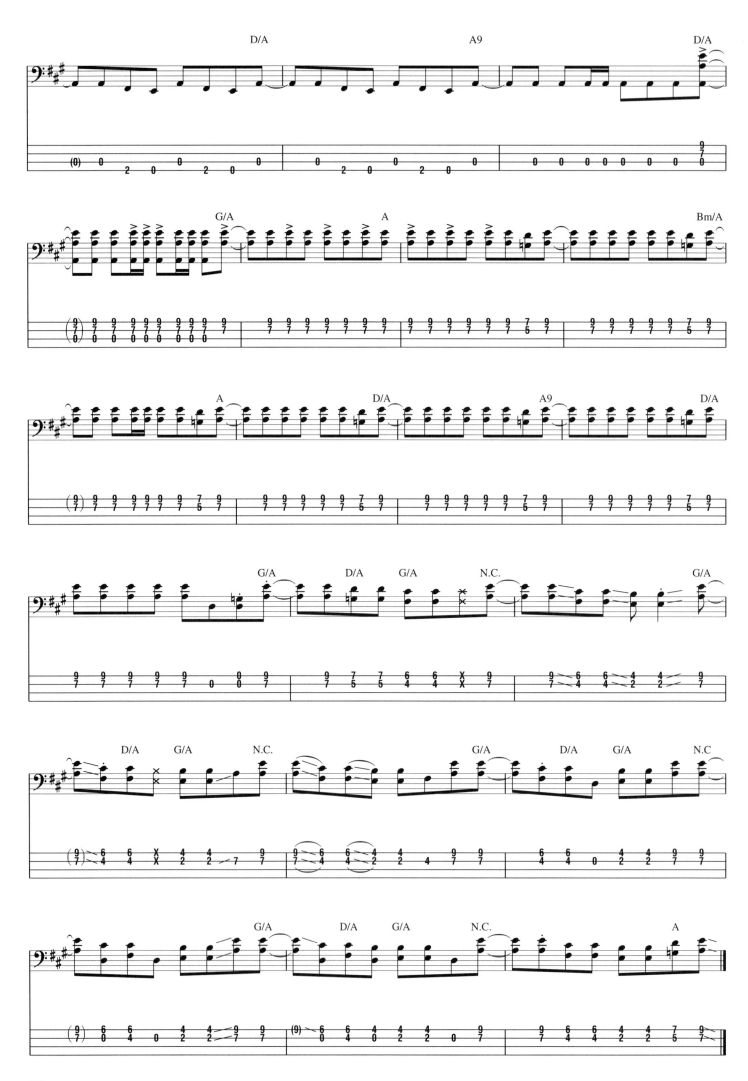

School Days

By Stanley Clarke

Copyright © 1980 Clarkee Music
All Rights Reserved

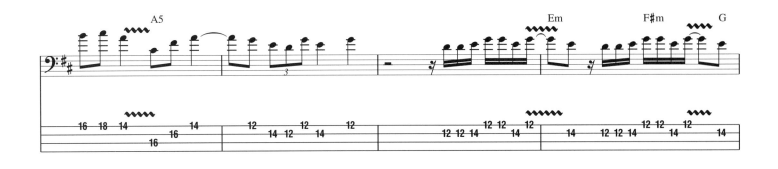

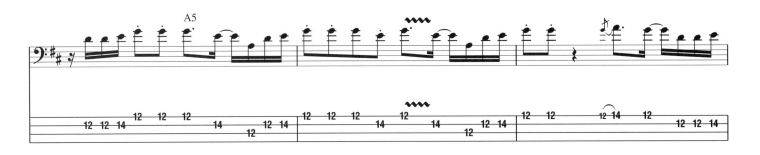

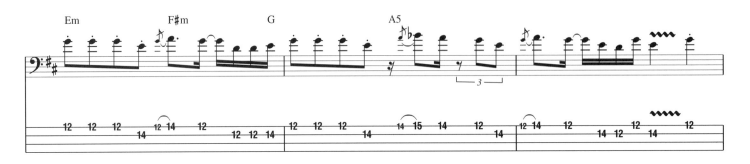

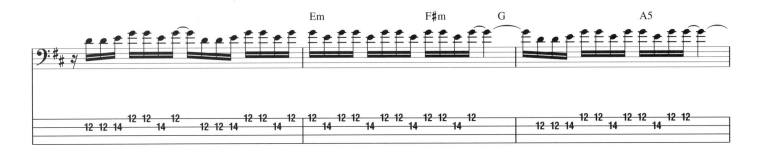

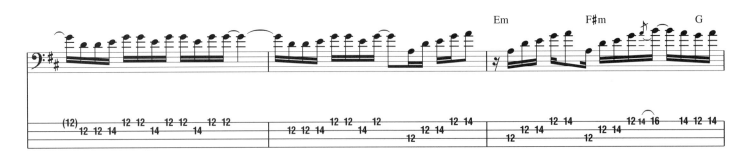

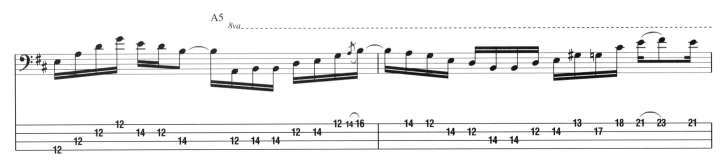

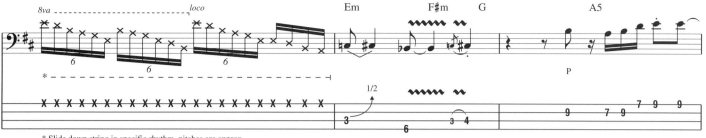

* Slide down string in specific rhythm, pitches are approx.

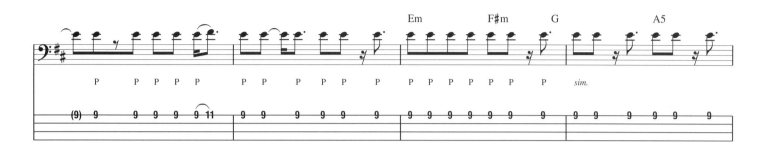

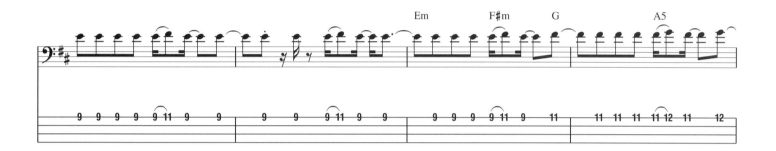

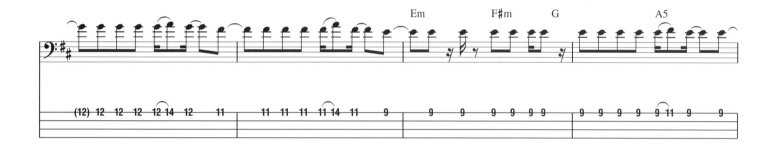

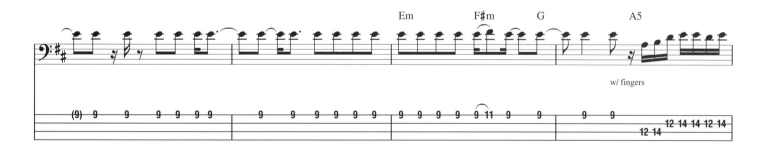

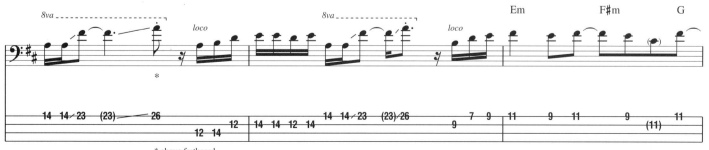

* above fretboard

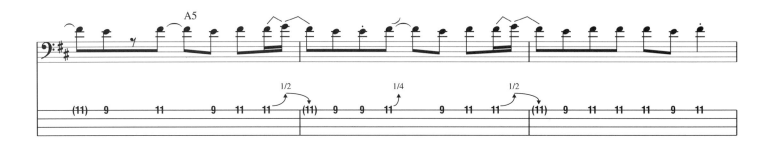

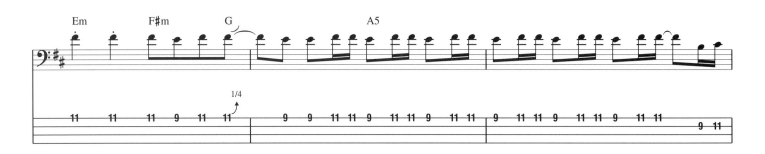

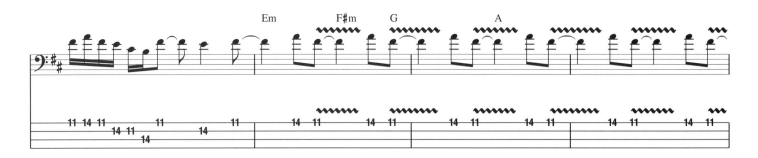

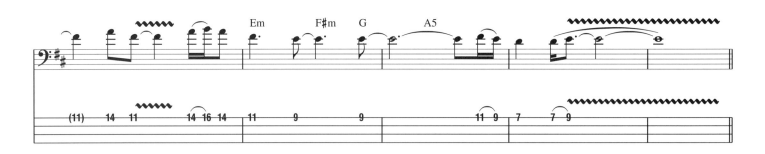

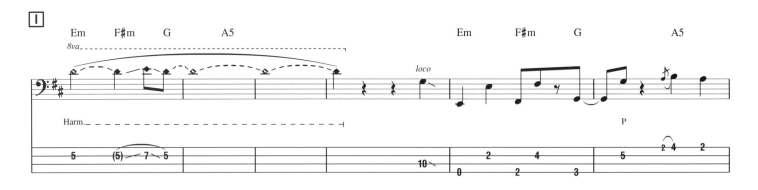

Silly Putty

By Stanley Clarke

* Key signature denotes E Mixolydian.

Copyright © 1977 Clarkee Music
All Rights Reserved

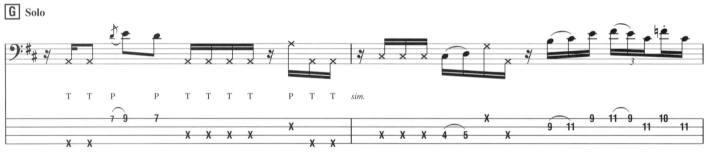

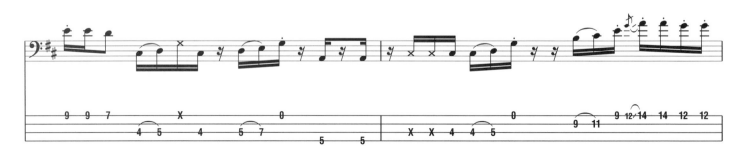

Song to John (Part II)

By Stanley Clarke

Copyright © 1975 Clarkee Music
All Rights Reserved

Stories to Tell

By Stanley Clarke

Copyright © 1988 Clarkee Music
All Rights Reserved

Time Exposure

By Stanley Clarke

Copyright © 1983 Clarkee Music
All Rights Reserved

⊕ Coda

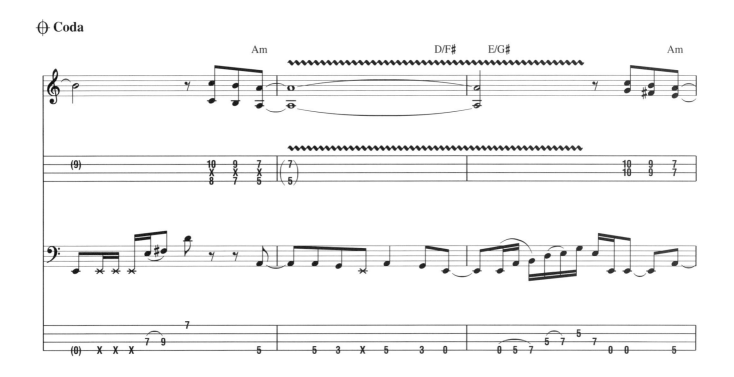

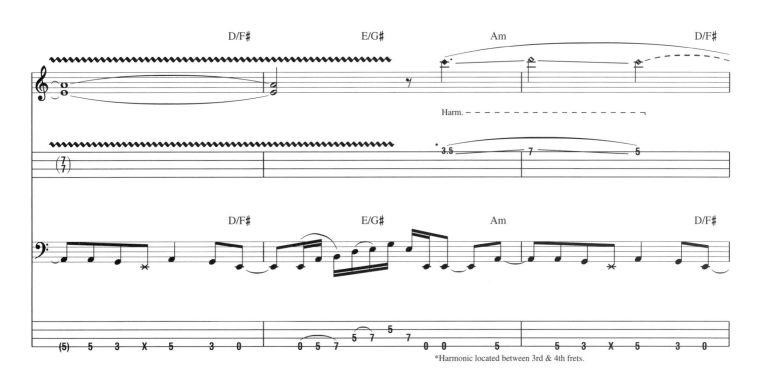

*Harmonic located between 3rd & 4th frets.

*Dbld. by bass (standard tuning) 2 octaves lower.

Play 6 Times & Fade

84

Vulcan Worlds

By Stanley Clarke

Copyright © 1974 Clarkee Music
All Rights Reserved

What If I Forget the Champagne

By Stanley Clarke

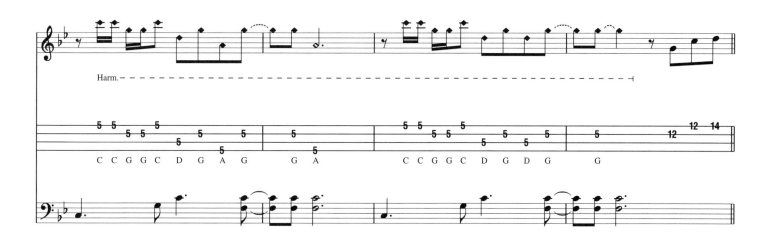

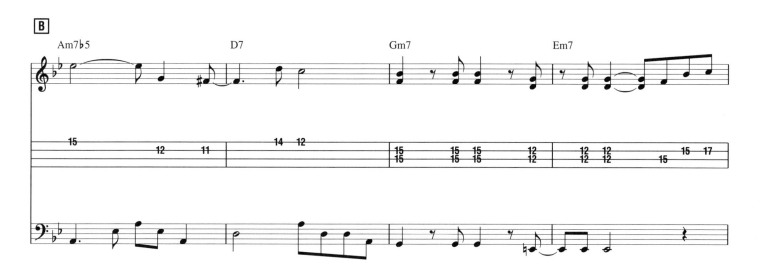

Copyright © 1993 Clarkee Music
All Rights Reserved

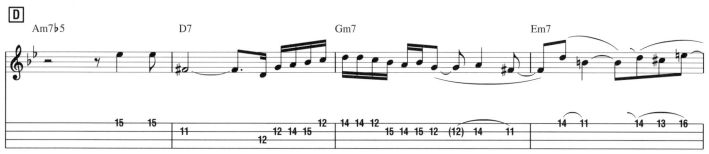

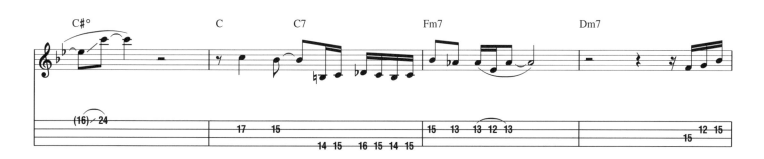

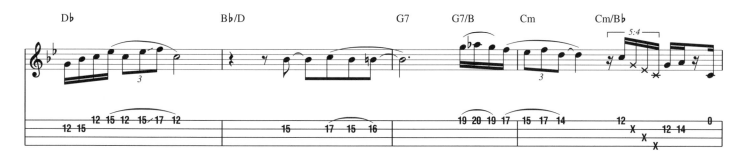

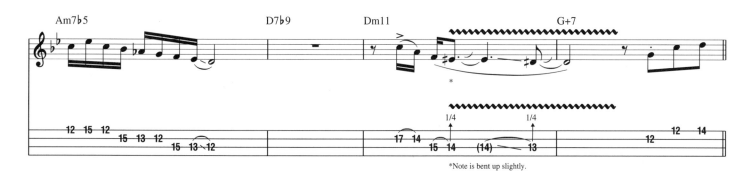

*Note is bent up slightly.